IT'S ONLY TV

Selected Poems: 2005 - 2011

Roger Aplon

...

I give the same attention to a crime as to an act of mercy
I vibrate the same to an idyllic landscape
And the spastic flashes of an electrical storm.
I diminish and exalt nothing
Confine myself to telling what I see.

From: **Nineteen-Thirty**
Poemas y Antipoemas (1938-1953)
Nicanor Parra
Translation by Miller Williams

For Zoe & Noa

With special thanks to Michael Knight and The Helene Wurlitzer Foundation of Taos, New Mexico for my two month residency when and where many of these poems were written

CONTENTS

TRUSTING PROVIDENCE

ENCOUNTERING DECEPTION

IT'S ONLY TV

ON THE EDGE

SPIDERS

Witness

The desert whispers & the lax winds are anxious. It never stops,

this nature, this inherent bartering for blood.

These eyes must see beyond
the ridge, the gorge, the dream, to where the rivers part, to those

who come willingly & without malice,
to begin & to be true.

She stands at the precipice smoking a local root & weeps,
calls to her mother who is no longer
but wishes her a long life,

to her father who never buried his guns & her brother lost
beyond redemption in the sands.
She will not hesitate, she

will not retreat . . . the months of grief bear witness,
attest to her commitment, to her belief
in restoration.

And when the hand comes from the cave to claim her,
she will not go easily, will not despoil
what's been bequeathed.

Her years may be short or long, who can tell, who can ever tell?
It's what she carries that matters,
the script & the bones.

Afghanistan 2009

TRUSTING PROVIDENCE

Something's Out There

I can feel its heat, smell the sweet scent of fresh sweat, hear the rustling in the fallen leaves.

A week has passed. I've yet to meet it face to face, to find its home or favorite hunting ground.

Oh, there've been signs: bark stripped from a young oak, flattened aunt hills, scattered strands of hair.

The day I stood at the window filming the stand of sun-draped trees across the road a long shadow,

the shape of a man or maybe a woman, fell across the field, when I turned to find the source, the space

was empty & the shadow gone. Last night, well after midnight, I awoke to a mewing or humming or

what could have been an animal trapped or a child weeping. I opened the door & the sound dissolved.

Today, I scouted the perimeter, found a kid's toy flute & a pyramid of small green & black stones. Tonight,

I'll sleep in the tree house I'd built for Chris & listen for her breathing & for the steps she never took &

set suspicion aside. Something's out there . . . waiting.

Donkey On A Cross

Above the city, splayed against a blue-black sky, where the big fish
compel the small, where

buffalo graze sodden-eyed their withers quivering, where a brotherhood
of ghosts

copulate in the dangerous grass & kids on meth dare to charge the
fortified fence . . .

A refuge for the fallen & infirm where those tarred & feathered might
cocoon in fresh skin, where

the cellist plucks arteries like strings, where she sculpts her teak vagina
stuffed with pins & nails & a stag-horn fern, where

hands reach through the wall to caress the passers-by, where a bag-lady
huddles in her winter shroud, where

boys, no more than twelve, harmonize their bamboo flutes & the priest
corrals the dancers for the last waltz

up the last hill to the garden that sprouts the stones.

He Awoke In The Dark

to his neighbor's wife
                                        yowling
like a cat in heat. It's Friday. Past midnight.

He lights a thin cigar & walks to the window.
The boy who plays the harmonica leans against the fence.
                                                                                Watching.
The moon twirls on its tether.
            The boy strokes his erection.
Her passionate song dissolves.
            The boy mouths his harp.

A bat darts across the moon.
The scent of honeysuckle warms the late-night air.

His cigar begins to shimmer like a butterfly – a Mourning Cloak – black,
edged in yellow lace.

Letting Go

Normal is a stormy engine quivering in the background, a backfiring
Dodge Ram grunting up the hill toward your old man's house.

The sun's obscured behind burlap & buildings loose from their tethers,
tankers hauling bad water, your last image lifted for evidence.

Our neighbors reel from the hint of blood while Zampano, our old
malamute, flops despondent on the daybed.

Not totally unexpected it's come to this, time again to pack the truck,
haul out the old canvas bags, box-up snapshots & history &

turn from the sea to the mountains . . . to the place where the ghosts of
renegades & rustlers sleep with the ancestors of Geronimo & Cochise,
where

the summer sun filters through the morning mist & Siberian Elms, where
coyote, deer & eagles still breathe free, where,

for the eighth time in as many years, I'll try to find a place, light up the
logs, pour a glass, open these weathered books & begin.

A Shower of dogs

Who could ever expect to survive a shower of dogs?

Anonymous

You who've never experienced the slightest doubt, beware
the snarling in the car / the smell of sweat in the mailbox.

These days are not only lessons in survival. There's a test being
conducted & you will be the last to know – the answer.

Bring a broom. There's work to be done & a harvest of Porcupines. Those
who return late from the trek cannot be expected to know the drill.

Comfort them but do not give sustenance. Remember. Thunder on the
hill is only that . . . the storm will appear when you least expect.

Open your eyes & breathe. This is not the time to panic.
Come Home. All is forgiven.

Tangier At Sundown

A man in black Jalaba descends the Kasbah's steps,
his edgy eyes mere slits in his bearded face.

There's the Muezzin's call to prayer, the musty scent
of wilting roses,

a lone drum at the desert's edge, clack, clack, clack
of dice in a box.

A rusty motor-launch tilts against its pier where a pair
of orange dogs sleep.

A woman in blue joins the man whose shredded flag
flips & flops above the cabin's door.

They were married in November, at sea in March &
lost to a needle in July.

Tonight he plans to revenge her violation, fuel a riot
to confuse pursuit, tonight

she'll dance naked with her pet cobra, milk venom
from their reluctant monk, tonight

they'll settle scores with Yitzhak, pledge a fresh start
for all who've confessed & ride high tide

to the straits where the current is swift & redemption
sleeps in the arms of a fractured moon.

You've Entered Their World

by water & wind & to these naked villagers you seem a God.

They toss you bouquets & oranges & you kiss their babies before
dawn finds you clothed

in a sparkling tie & Armani suit squatting in the muck at the edge
of the swamp

where you've come to gnaw the thing in your hand that drips blood
on your chest with every bite.

Is it the heart you'd stolen from the ripe baboon or it is your own heart
the one bristling with magic

that calls all to be whole again?

Trusting Providence

Where's that cunning gambler who'd broken bread with the devil & matched dice with the hanged man,

the urgent swimmer who'd claimed the Hellespont [or was it merely an interlude in the Adriatic],

the shattered lover who climbed too high & lost his footing on the steep cliff of unappreciated lust?

He's here, broken but alive, licking his wounds & trusting providence to bring him around the bend

before the cut over the eye or the ruptured spleen makes him call it quits. Not long ago, one foot

before the other had him marching in circles meeting himself at the crossroads hands clasped

in prayer [or is it fear, they look so much alike]. Today finds him climbing into the last frame

where the group portrait will be displayed. He's the one on the far left with the forced grin &

the glass of wine – a Rioja, his favorite & that of the Kings of Spain.

From His Vantage Point at the Bow

the captain calls the markers.

He's chosen to steer into the typhoon where there are only shadows
& no miracles to defend.

Those left at the dock speak well of the man with one good arm who
reefed the main & was never seen again.

The further they walked from town the greater their need to confess, he
with his stories of failed courage & she without hope.

Arms raised in surrender, they were marched to the ravine, shot & left like
laundry to molder in the rain.

Remember me to those with sorrow & to those without conscience leave
the flayed skin of his daughter's goat.

Survival has its price.

After Their Landing

she led the way to the bridge & the worn path to the temple.

By nightfall, she'd scrubbed her dirty linen & sworn vengeance on those
in red who'd refused to carry his corpse.

In the dim morning light she fashioned a shroud from the skin of a
jackal, his coffin from an abandoned oil drum.

It wasn't enough to know he'd be planted under his favorite Banyan
Tree
near the sheer cliffs above the sea. No.

There must be singing & dancing & a flurry of naked women to mime
his rituals of sex & beyond

there must be jasmine tea & whiskey, poems & stories from the dark.

The Woman Who Sleeps With The Devil

rises after midnight, smokes a thin cheroot & lines her eyes with the blood of his defiant guests.

She grows orchids in her greenhouse, distills rye whiskey & harvests the neighbor's cats for stew.

The woman who sleeps with the devil never travels far from home, refuses invitations & paints her windows black.

She will not speak of her past but hints at a rendezvous with an aunt who guards the family bible &

brings her souvenirs: a rabbit's foot her father cured, her mother's ashes in a blue porcelain urn, a tape of her sister's last words.

In winter, when his furnace heats their home, she spins wool to yarn & weaves his exotic capes & shrouds.

The woman who sleeps with the devil has learned to identify renegades, shanghai slavers, generals & executioners.

She's combed our streets for charlatans, those who sell the trinkets of god's army to unsuspecting tourists.

They're a team, last seen wandering our fields hand in hand, she with a shovel & he with his torch & hook.

No one dares climb the hill to their rooms. We suspect anarchy & treason but will never interfere. Their privacy is our salvation.

The Usual Suspect

I was born in a dream, he said & smiled
at the inquisitive camera.

His silver teeth glistened in the afternoon sun,
his eyes black holes.

Mother hangs around my neck, he said flashing her
blue onyx locket.

His jaw-line rigid as honed steel, arms crossed,
fingers knotted.

Father flew to oblivion, he said & chortled
when he said it.

As he swaggered off, tossing bits of toast
to the sparrows that followed,

we marveled at his command of all things holy
& without merit,

of his whispering & awkward gestures that signaled
a storm coming.

The Man & The Moon

The moon cracks wide & out spits the bitter
fruits of passion

Along the wall where couples fondle & share
their beer

he squirms & sips the expensive vodka he
allows his arrogance &

something, maybe a flutter in his gut or the
sweat that clings, tells him he has no country

& tells him no one will open the door for the
stranger with the complicated eye &

a passion for silence.

Well before dawn he's gone to arrange his
bed in the loft

where portraits of the hunted hang with bones
of dogs that have stood their ground

where he cooks his meal in a tin, drinks sour
wine from a dusty bottle & kisses her

who comes in the broken hours to bathe him
& stroke him back

where visions of home & honor are only dust
on the vacant shelves.

I Saw Her Through The Mist

She wore a red scarf & held a black cat in her arms. We were married on Tuesday & divorced on Thursday. There were Robins in the yard. Her cat slept next to my head & made a meal of one or two. I can't remember. That was August. It wasn't that she hated me. Or me her. No. It was weather. A simple fact. Something most won't admit. Don't you see? She was winter: cold, brittle & honest. I was summer: romantic, hot & rampant with lies.

At Night All Cats Are Grey

1

We move as one / knowing nothing of origins.
Each rendezvous a test / bruised knuckles & blood in the eye.

I wake among polished stones / you beside the river dressed in ivy.
There's a red Ferrari & a plump mare saddled.

Someone begins a prayer / takes your hand & snaps a picture.
I'm the last to offer condolences.

2

In the shadow-life I hunt for a memory that will trigger your return,
guard the weaving beads that are your monument.

3

Listen: there's the hiss & scratch in the waning dark & the shriek
that tells of rank deeds done.

It may not have been what you wanted or expected. Similar moments
have been dissected & the organs tossed.

Smell: distinct scent of toasted hair / & eye / tooth / the sucking sound
of their copulation.

ENCOUNTERING DECEPTION

She's Wed Her body

She's wed her body to the wind & into the arms of her mourning father.
Poor Rebecca. Pobrecita

Year one brought the whip & their neighbor's fears, cool nights with
branding irons & puckered flesh.

By the second, she suffered amnesia & deserted him to wander in search
of origins & memory, to hunt

the monkish writer with yellow eyes, the soldier with his loving gun, the
tattooed & muscled thief.

Today, she's bundled in sheep's wool, driven over the ice to her new
home beside the great canyon.

There's a silver cigarette between her teeth & an expectation of revival. In
the pale morning light,

her skin's alive, the mountains shimmer & glow. She slips a gloved hand
between her legs & begins

the rhythmic ritual that has served to calm these days, these years of
grief: quiet & dark where,

one by one, the shades appear to tease & taunt, to mimic the confessor &
his hint of liberation. There's one

chance left. Bind them close as blood or sweep them out the door, they're
your treasured relics & your curse.

There's no turning back. The choice is yours.

In Memory We Find Our Way

Today she wears Asia behind her ears & Spain between her breasts.
She's traveled far with strangers, prefers her morning walk alone.

Today, she stoops to pick a yellow rose that she fastens to her
flowing hair. Today, she will be reminded of the Budapest of her

youth & the man who rode the silver bicycle & the other who
followed her to the bridge & held her back.

Today, she will ride the train from Prague & work in the bakery &
meet Andre & today she will climb the hill to his house

where his brother will take her & she will fight back & lose &
when he has finished with her body

she will be left & . . . & now the clouds form as they often do & she's
on a steamer bound for New York & there are yellow flowers & . . .

Her Scar

lit up the night like a hot tongue licking across her belly.
She could hear the eighteen-wheelers cursing the ruts above the Hudson.

In November she'd resolved to bury his sword & pistol, leave the myth
of the hurricane behind, to oblige the wrestler.

That was then. This is now. Her scar reminds her of revenge.
The boy who came to the door last night left a bad taste.

She washed it away with Boodles & tonic, scrubbed the skin raw.
What was she thinking?   There's that kissing cat again.

Before the avalanche, before the whiskey rebellion, before monotony
there were the races & dress-up with high hats & roses.

Every time she came around they'd tell lies about that time – that time
she was whole, not like the broken banker who was her father.

Today began with steamed eggs, tomatoes & a nasty sore throat.
If only the nights were not impossible. If only nature could be trusted.

Wish Us Luck

She opens the door & stares into the moonlit street. There's
the hum of cicadas & the click, click, click of crickets.

She's been like this, hands limp, wandering eyes, skin a pale blue.
Subject to interpretation. Like the time in Peoria

when she lost the truck in the fog, or the time in Wichita when John
cussed the cop & they both did time. That's changed too.

These are her days of grace. Bountiful. Acres of corn in spite of excess
in the vineyards: syrup too thick . . . too sweet to swallow . . . & there's

her machine in the house of horrors, created for the dummies & the frogs,
her bestiary with alligators & ocelots, (never-mind) bubblegum &
kerosene.

Where's her mother now? Where's daddy's ghost, with all its hate &
resolve? Bury them in the heap where the snake-babies live.

There'll be peace in the trees . . . maybe . . . muted fire in the hole.
Wish us luck. What's tomorrow without repentance?

After A Fitful Night & Friday Morning Jazz @ KRZA 89.7 Taos, NM

Faint echo of a full moon rocking in its cradle, a conversation with a young girl about sex & where they could have it . . . & there she was naked & willing & after exploring her body with his eyes & hands & mouth she disappeared into the night & he was left with a long drive down a dark road where even the moon couldn't go. That was the beginning followed by an argument with the gate keeper, barking dogs & a climb up a hill to a monastery where a man & woman waited to tell his fortune before sending him back for a shrunken skull & a necklace of human teeth.

After fumbling the ball & a wrong turn he ends up in a painter's studio where his young mother is modeling nude holding a ripe orange in one hand & a rifle in the other. The painter stands him against the wall & demands his mother shoot the fruit from his head – he hears the shot but is already down the stairs driving fast to the city-limits where Tanya waits with a skiff & her pet ocelot. The rest is too murky to see clearly except their ride through rough water to the harbor where someone hands her a blank check & him a glass of chilled Dutch gin garnished with a lemon twist & one small green dilled tomato.

Where It All Began

A Meadow Lark with straw in its beak darts between rows of ripening grapes.

Dry hills roll away to mesquite & sage. A rider-less horse outlined against a cloudless sky.

We've met here, where it all began, to harvest the remnants of desire.
Try our hand at remorse. Maybe / tame the crow

we'd swallowed in rehearsal. It's never been easy. For either of us.
We're not predictable, never could be trusted to hold the center.

It was too often warm wine or curdled milk. Each encounter a challenge:
who would be first to fortify a beachhead

before the war began in earnest. How many takes were left on the cutting-room floor, how many kids lost in those early skirmishes?

Today we've chosen to begin with knives. In case we're unsuccessful, a clean cut is preferred to blatant butchery.

I've offered the number eight. It's said to be supportive & relatively neutral.
You've held out for six – a deal-buster for sure.

Maybe it's the setting. Too bucolic? No place to plant rage or deceit?
Can we ever find peace?

You suggest the heat of Bangkok to have it out – the din & chaos might be a better fit. We've always thrived on both.

We'll need tickets. I'll arrange the buy. Pack your Glock – There'll be
no other chance.

Encountering Deception

It begins (as do all dreams) with a gesture / finger thrust above the crowd & ends with words meant to lacerate the spine.

In between, you may be forced to leap a pit of boiling tar, spear his eye with a well-placed dart, stow-away in a submarine.

He'll not be the wiser. Oh. Yes. He may infer treason but will settle for disrespect & when he's ready might even extend his hand. But don't

be conned by piety. Never trust a seemingly open door. When he offers to conduct the ensemble suggest a duel.

& if it's fire you desire, insist he marry his thrice-bedded sister. Remind him of his promise. It's then you must prepare to pay.

But if it's a tranquil afternoon you're after, take the first ship south. Draw a hot bath & for your sake & sanity, don't ever look back.

The Man Waits

where dark water streams down rusted walls & the odor of death taints the air.

He cradles his small bindle of clothes, his unfinished manuscript, dinner in a paper bag.

She's been gone a month & he bites his lips thinking of his pathetic gestures – clasping her close those last nights.

Where was he when she needed to talk of the dark stranger in her dream or the horse that ran with her & would not stop?

Where was he when she called his name & heard (only) the echo of her own voice through their empty rooms?

The juice of their life together, like the steady drip from a cracked pipe, urged repair. There were times

they'd tried, much like the kiss before the storm, when mourning will not bring back what's been lost.

Today, as he lifts his eyes to scan the fading light he sees her, once again, walking away,

ensconced in her blood-red shroud, permanently
out of reach.

Deserted

The underpass is home to the abandoned and stinks of shit.
Those who come to live out their time do not. Not
at the beginning.

I see them in the locker room, men with callused hands and darkened arms, men who've worked & now cannot. There is none.

They come to shower. To be clean. To honor their integrity. To save what little is left. They don't speak to strangers. Will not look me in the eye.

On Sunday, when the Y is closed, where do they go for sanctity, for soap & clean water? That's when they wish for rain or a river near by,

somewhere, out of sight, somewhere, anonymous. In the underpass you claim what you can, share what's found, remember

privacy is sacred, sanity is simple, as crucial as a well-honed blade.

IT'S ONLY TV

Across The Street

an old man walks from his sitting-room to his balcony & begins to cry.
His house faces the western quadrant. We shall never know exactly why.

They keep us this way. Not knowing the contours of our neighbor's lives.
It's for the best they tell us & shutter our windows if we inquire too often.

Some say the old man lost his wife last Monday, others, a daughter raped.
Another suggests there was a son - gone bad or maybe lost to war.

The mad woman with one good eye & a crutch tried to trace her lost dog.
On Wednesday she found it hung by its neck from her bronze doorknob.

Nothing is as it seems. Our minister's not been seen since December.
It's rumored he left with the laundress who'd run afoul of the general.

If time were right & an offer made, most would find the means to go.
There've been those who have / found in the woods eaten by rats.

If it were his wife or daughter or son who will he have left to mourn?
Most have learned to take comfort in the passing of those most dear.

Joaquin's son Jose was delivered home today in a blue plastic bag.
The VFW plans to reward the grieving family with a traditional fiesta.

To question 'who holds the reins' is to ask for confrontation or worse.
Is it best to live quietly in your relegated space & tend your vines?

I'll never succumb to breast-beating over spilled blood or loss of love.
When my turn comes to walk the ramparts, I'll do it with eyes wide shut

There's a time to rage & a time to weep. I've lost the will for either.
Bury me soon – before I'm asked to believe again.

Between Here & There

A hyena is seen to mate a silver fox - wolves pace behind the bamboo break

On the hospital's terrace one man whittles balsam dogs while another plays the Jew's harp & practices walking on his shiny new legs.

It's Wednesday. The phones are dead. It's the day after the lowered flag, the day the prisoners escaped.

Between here & there the latrines have overflowed, those left to clean house barter guns for opium.

In the distance, across the field of snow, what appears an army on the march is merely a swarm of the hungry & the fearful.

The Man Who Lives Underground

no longer wanders the streets of our town but gathers what he needs in the night alone.

The floor of his tunnel is slippery, it's the grime from above, a slim stream but steady.

He respects time, is cautious, hauls his waste bucket by bucket, his meals bag by bag.

Winter brings him various visitors: a young & lithe Thai girl who cooks him
hot stuffed buns,

a dragon master from Bombay who smokes hashish & warns of assassins that come soon,

Barbara, the dyke corporal from Portland, who'd escaped the war & lives to find her God.

By June he's alone again, an occasional visit from the mayor's wife to sustain him.

She'd been his father's mistress in another life & now comes to his empty bed wanting.

The man who lives underground has no use for politics or paradise. He has made his peace.

Oh, there's still the turbulence: memory & sleep haunted by her ghost, the pistol's crack,

hours of interrogation, Ambien & Zoloft, years of scouring her history for those vague clues.

He plans to leave this fall. Santiago or Havana. He'll be anonymous & secretly safe.

They've told him this, those voices he hears while he hacks at the walls burrowing down,

excavating, vein-by-vein, what's left of his salvation - his brief refuge & his silent hell.

In Our Town

After midnight there are dead sheep in the street, old men towing caskets & buckets of human waste. There're feral dogs & feral cats that hunt for the slow & infirm.

After midnight in this country of women, drained of all but their bag of skin, you can pay to watch her being flayed or their hanging or his castration; most forms of ingenious torture.

After midnight our town is quiet except for the rumble of metal wheels on cobblestones when the gypsies emerge from their caves, ride to the fountain to drink & wash & fuck on the warm grass.

After midnight you'll find a few punks on the dike at the end of my street swigging gin & beer & telling stories of plunder & mayhem & puking their guts on the rocks. & as the day breaks

there's the odor of roasted corn & piss & you'll wrap yourself in your great black shroud & whistle your way down the boulevard & when you reach the crossroads, if your smart, you'll turn left & never look back.

Iraq – Year Three

The Feather & The Rock

In this dream he's surrounded by a pack of yowling dogs & no one responds to his calls. The hills move closer. A thick & steady rain . . . The clap & swish of wings

It's been like this,

night after night, a subtle devouring of spirit, a fever that grows more fierce each hour . . . & these visions from his past:

his brother running up a hill into a rain of fire, a pen of pigs gorge on the body of a goat, a butcher's knife

in the hands of a kid with no eyes, an angry snake coiled around its clutch of eggs, his son's name on a head-stone written in blood.

It wasn't always.

There were seven years of plenty when his celebrated paintings captured the angst & horror of the war & seven years of sorrow from which

he keeps an uncut rock of lapis to remind him of the dark blue nights of the summers in the Morocco of his youth, a golden

pheasant's feather to remind him of the glow & texture of your smooth, tan skin on the beach in Tangier the day you said goodbye.

To Live & Die Alone

"The mountain opens & where a river once ran you'll leave your life"

The guards have called a halt.
It's you who must open the cavern, release the priests that trade in favors.

Our colonel kneels in his doorway, recites the prayer as it came to him:
'Marry me my sister & I pledge to awaken the sleepers among us.'

No one speaks of the incarcerated led to slaughter behind the house.
No one is allowed inside with he who is charged with the executions.

Speak to me of death & reward in heaven & I will laugh in your teeth.
Speak to me of love & whisper war & I spit on your grave.

Celebrating Departure

The key no longer fits the lock. It's the work of the managers.
They're efficient / won their medals in Baghdad & Fallujah.

*

The captain, driving far ahead, says they must set aside desire,
earn the right to sleep the good sleep.

"Nightmares aside, she's a ghost in need of sustenance."

*

Wait. Let me think. Yes. Toss in a slow fuck in the sun, bodies
on the lawn & you've begun the novel: "Lust Versus Impatience"

*

On the hill, young women warn of fools who juggle dynamite.
Others, drinking in the corner café, toast the urge for revenge.

*

As light eases in the west someone bangs your door, demands
a place to sleep & your daughter for sex.

Grandma slips to the basement where the axe is kept.

*

Now is the time to hit the road. Gather herbs & berries.
Feed the earth. Remain engaged – willing . . .

Days & Men That Corrupt Our Soul

When you speak of them remember their destitute wives . . . kids buried in the dunes.

All those hours they'd conjured triumph for the faithful & torture for the unenlightened.

Remember the voiceless among us, those who speak in riddles, the muscular

& hesitant who roam their estates like wild boar / guns drawn & ample time to dig the trenches soon

to be the graves . . .

*

These will be called 'The Days of Silence.'

You've encountered them. Possibly in your own home, asleep in a closet you haven't searched for years.

How careful of you – how cool. Still – here they are – waiting.

& the first to open the trap door is the first to be free.

*

When you speak

note the inevitability of their reproduction / holding a fat check: each offspring a cipher in their wallet / their table well set . . . &

*

Witness:

The frost-bitten & sleep-deprived who haunt the prison halls hungry for a vision of sky & a taste of time without fear.

Witness:

Their fleets of armor that ignore the condemned to trap salvation in the wings where it awaits the parted sea.

*

When men with baseball bats & secret clearance enter your house they will clean your teeth by removing your mouth.

The two who carry your body to the door will be dressed in white to signify truth, honesty & the way to heaven.

*

Here are those who relish absolute power – count them. Refuse to settle (as have others) . . . demand retribution.

*

Henry. He who dwells in the labyrinth of souls lost to pride. Knows no other way. It's genetic. Arrogance breeds contempt.

When a Jew is chosen to carry the flag of honor & dishonors it. Shame comes to us all.

*

When the call went out across the land to free the enslaved minds it was he who knotted the cloth, chained the wrists & spoke not a word.

*

Never Again.

*

Take my hand. We'll walk to the edge of the cliff where we can watch the city in flames.

It's not pleasant. No. But, if you squint you'll see the fires are only barking dogs. The city can be saved.

Call off the dogs. Tell them what you know of falling bodies & the actions of haunted men.

*

Through it all, my son asks to hear a human voice. A voice that may, at last, speak truth.

A proclamation. Word from 'On High.' Not from those carpet-baggers, those insidious preachers of the 'Word.' No!

Disavow them all. Cull the chaff from the seed. Renew your license. Open your mouth, speak loudly . . . without fear.

The Woman Aaron

speaks of deserts: of oases & life, of honey dates & oranges, of quicksand & hunters on horseback. The desert is like that,

life in one hand, death in the other. It's been so since the first camel, the first scorpion, the first enigmatic nomad.

She also speaks of hyenas (driven mad by memories), of tanks & phosphorus bombs & burns that never heal,

of missiles & mortars & vultures hunkering. Today is day eighteen of desert war, war that began forty years ago, or

five thousand seven hundred sixty nine years ago. It cloaks the land of milk & honey in its quilt of blood.

She speaks now of the fearful (huddled in shattered doorways) & the broken (missing eyes & arms), the demented

(mumbling under blankets of bones) & of the heroic (clawing though rubble seeking the lost, the dying & the dead).

Gaza Israel 1-13-2009

It's Only TV

She sips her red wine & watches him. It's the final day of the offer & there are thousands waiting in the wings. Waiting
for her decision.

She's been at it for months. This rehabilitation. This resurrection. This charade. Complete with sobs & tears.
Kleenex.

& he's followed, refilling her glass, planting kisses in the furrows, massaging every opportunity, muscle & bone,
skin & moist sex.

On her last trip to Egypt she rented a young man for the afternoon, taught him how she liked to be touched, where
& with what.

In Marrakech it was a young woman & hot oil. He was there too with his eager fingers, improbable & passionate
Chimpanzee.

At this writing, they've not been seen for a week. The documents don't lie. There are orders to fill: baguettes & bayonets.
Ammunition.

She'd always been capable of magic. Remember her disappearance from the box with the sword, snatching the bloody ace
from the deck?

Two months have passed & not a word. Even after an arm was found in the alley, a hand in the deserted street. The dead
Chihuahua. Even after

the exploding tower, four feathers, appeal for blood & organs, nurses crawling in the rain, Marcia's rape.
In this town,

few things matter. We'll get along. They were only window dressing, a good laugh, money well spent.
Let it go . . . It's only TV.

The Part of The Gypsy Girl

will be played by her twin, the one with one brown eye & one blue. She'll carry a guitar & dress in a velvet coat. Her smile will be painted green, her frown a pale pink. When she enters the secret room there'll be men with drawn swords & automatic pistols to guard her every move. & where she walks there'll be corpses to name & caskets she must number & bless. & when she's ensconced in the limousine she must not be tempted to kiss the general who sits at her right or the queen who sits on her left. & when they arrive at their inevitable stop she'll be carried to her room where they'll extract her eyes & replace them with the eyes of the goat who oversees war. It's then she'll be led to edge of the town where she'll be left to roam our valleys & mountains & sing of all she has seen.

The Old Man Speaks

I have no brothers. My father left long ago as ashes & smoke. Mother too. I don't make demands, nor should I.

I chat with those that come in the night, muse at their handwringing, all those gestures of guilt & remorse. I trust no one.

We walked the same roads, drank from the same wells, ate the same rabbits & squirrels, shat in the same hole. How quickly they forget.

It was the winter of '57. Food had run low. Hank died in his sleep. We'll gut him & preserve the carcass. Opportunities arise. Mistakes are made.

I think of the kids we rescued only to have that bastard Bob rape the girl & sell the boy to the gypsies. Scum rises. War will do that to a man.

I think of nurse Sharon & her incredibly high, round ass, the way she flaunted it & wondered why all the wives . . . well, you can imagine.

& the incident with the neighbor we caught filming our maneuvers. Didn't have a chance. Not against the six of us. A dark stain remained.

When it was over, it was over. Maury counted what was left and bagged the rest. We weren't good at goodbyes . . . Semper Fi

We'd returned, cold & broken, brittle & firm. Whenever the sun rose, we'd muscle our chairs down the ramp & into its warmth . . .We'll never forget.

ON THE EDGE

He Tucks The Morning Line In His Hip Pocket

& begins the long trek home. There's not much time before he must leave for the south.

In Alexandria there's a woman who sews & embroiders silk shrouds. They are her gifts for all who have ever passed her door.

We encounter him after he's lost twenty pounds & wrestles drunks behind a rooming-house in Baltimore.

Those who've been chosen are unaware of her special gift.

When their time is up the signed forms must appear on the desk of the town magistrate.

The postman arrives at his door to deliver the letter from Prague & is met with curses & a cocked pistol.

In January. In Paris. In a small bar. There sits a man without a nose sipping from a cup of absinthe.

The woman who sent the letter to Simon has recently inherited a million dollars from her son's estate.

His daughter sits cross-legged on the floor tossing the dice he'd whittled from the hip of their dead cat.

From Baltimore there's a quick train to Philadelphia where a man everyone calls a hermit has built a shrine to the 'god' he calls: EX.

She informs Simon of the need to reinvent her life without either of them. There's a banknote for a thousand dollars enclosed.

If you choose to visit Philly you'll find my Aunt Esther selling tickets but you must not buy them from her – especially, not from her.
When the dice come up red & black you have a stiff shot at success & if they are both white you will invite your own death

Go back to your car & west to Pittsburgh where the money has been well laundered & the steaks are flown fresh from Missouri.

Never play too long at the same table. You are well-known here & the trackers will find you soon enough.

In the south. In a hotel run by a retired mortician. There lives a woman with one golden eye.

Go to her. She will see you now.

He's Checked Into A Hotel

where he lounges, smoking thin Cohiba's, sipping eight-year-old Kentucky straight & dreaming of those calm,
sultry nights in Juarez.

It's been a long trip back, fused to the usual suspects: mom & her weathered excuses for drinking gin all day the pain
the nausea, the . . . &

Charley with his bum heart & once quick hands fumbling the cards still bent on taking it to the suckers on Fremont St.
the way he used to. &

Liza of the raven hair & purple eyes who could twist him like no other sucking up his juice, leaving him a fleshy,
fumbling shell.

The habit of those little cuts was back. He pours another glass. Once he'd walked across Death Valley on a dare & made it
with water to spare.

Last night in Dallas he'd set himself free; ditched the car & told them to head north on their own.
The bourbon

tasted good, best since that sweet Anejo in San Juan. He remembered the chubby mystic turning
up the clown

card followed by the hanged man & how the room hushed & the seer's face turned a peculiar shade
of blue.

Whatever possessed him to open the gate, to barter his daughter, to follow the piper down the well?
Will there be time

to cross the bridge again, to drink clear water, to shed his blistered skin?
Will he ever see a morning
without rain?

If You Listen At His Door

you might hear the staccato chant & cry of a man lost in his past whose body is tormented bone by bone, a man recently arrived

with one small bag who paid for his meals with dated bills & his room with a stone the professor would buy.

You might encounter a frail girl asleep on a palette beside the remnants of his formal coat & tie & the skin

of a cat – withered in winter – among dead bees & birds asleep in the spider's web.

As the day draws down you'll find yourself in the presence of the caretaker who'll offer a cigar & a deck of cards.

You must avoid the smoke but be sure to concentrate as he deals your hand, his face-cards marked – a history of mayhem & murder – &

beware the naked lady who opens her legs & offers her nesting snake to the unsuspecting – she will enchant &

follow to your private door, unlock your heart & dine on what's left of the man you were.

Man On Fire

The smoke came fast, a funnel above the ridge,
swept to the valley below.

A lone rider, his hand raised in salute, drives the herd
before the flames.

The horse market in Rabat teems with savage monkeys,
with kids who cut

cards to know who will be the next to climb beyond
hope.

Sand bodies dance & swirl like dervishes – erupt
like soldiers blown to bits.

The rider drives on – breathing fire – raining
fire – fire in his eyes.

His flames sweep to the sea – golden & green,
his horses screaming.

Postcards

On it the sea was blue & green & dissolved when I lifted it to my lips expecting you to appear & kiss me, take me in your arms, bring me to my bed – hold me against the dark.

*

I must tell you, I found a goat with a broken leg, a father who turned his back, a mother confused by the light & . . . did you mean to leave for the month or just that Saturday night?

*

I've decided to catch a train to Pittsburgh, to apply for work in a factory that polishes bearings. You might find the weather more exciting in June. Take care & remember to pray for thunder & the opportunity for rain.

*

What was sacred yesterday has fallen off my desk. For all I know your wedding came off without a hitch (ha-ha). Do you plan to raise sheep or was that a joke too? Remember me to mother & salt the wounds.

*

To escape your past turn right at the last house on the road north. Action is best taken on a full stomach. Be sure to refill the lamps & butter your buns. Tony left this morning. Even the gulls are laughing.

On The Edge

The maple leaves have begun to turn. There's been no rain.

On Valencia Street the toothless beggar snoozes in the shade of the painter's awning.

Boys & girls from the parochial school around the corner flirt & kiss in the park across the way. It's 3 o'clock

She'd announced the end last week & he's been drunk ever since. Begins juicing before even the alarm.

The car she drives is fast, comfortable, filled with ghosts & goes only where she directs.

The fables that sprung-up around the table tell of lovers crossed & the terror of a gun in the wrong hands. It's Midnight

No one seems to notice the singer in the flowered slip who's slit her wrists & dances slowly marking her way.

In New York City at 4 AM the lady of the house cannot sleep. She wanders & sips her potion,

the one with vodka, mint & sassafras . . . the one with the black seed at the center.

5 AM & all is quiet on front street except for the staccato slap/slap/slap (thigh against thigh) as the neighbor's daughter entertains her man.

& if we look for him, the boozer, he's asleep on his fire escape. In his dream, he has little left . . .

Sunrise Soon

The Clock Strikes One

She's asleep. There's a black Angora cat under her window. Two sheep in the yard. All asleep.

& where is the shepherd? The one with the golden voice? The one who steals her dreams, who swims

between her legs, claws the skin at the back of her neck, ransacks her house of beeswax & hair? He

who stuffed her dresser with deceit, her pantry with poisoned wine, her chest with a fractured plum.

Tonight she wakes. Intent. She must strike out, stalk the vacant rooms, settle the score.

There'll be no retreat. Only attack. She stops. Listens at the last door. Pistol cocked. Teeth on fire.

It will be now.

The Cage

She shares the cage with The Man On Fire & The Drowning Man, but not for long. There will be room for more & more will come:

From the peak, an Amazon with blue-black hair, a muscular juggler juggling machetes, a monk with shrunken skull & tiger's teeth.

It's no different than it's always been say those missing limbs & eyes & one, half a face. They tell of the butchery &

the struggle for a place in the cage where the butchery is done. & they tell of the survivors who've ruled the country &

now, She's won her place & will sever the head of the white beast & drink the spilt blood & in her time

she'll chose a successor who will fight her to the end & the winner will be first & a man will come who has

ridden the beast & carries cards to tell your fortune & you will leave with him & only one will return.

He Wondered Aloud

voice like a blade through bone.
If I go this way will she be waiting?

& she, wishing she could ignore her seductive ghosts,
hides in the wings, nurses the ache of severance.

No matter. Their past was choked with seaweed,
empty envelopes, dial tones & masturbation.

& what of her husband, his wife? Think of them
as broken bicycles, she'd said. Junk, he'd thought.

& whatever happened to that trip to the border,
their belated renewal – passion rekindled?

Will there be another time? None left to waste.
It's the right decision. No matter how ironic.

Leave the door ajar, remove the blinders.
What has been will be no longer. Wait!

There's another way . . . The midnight train,
car fifteen. It carries the caskets & our history.

All will be disclosed en route. Even the unasked
will be answered. We owe it to ourselves.

To hell with the hangers-on. They didn't dare to risk,
didn't dare to touch

the white-hot moon.

The Conversation

I miss you, she said, sweeping away her old insulation.

I miss you too, he said, & wonders what that might mean.

I remember your mouth, she said, your soft lips & how you left me . . .

He rubs the dark onyx charm at his neck, sucks down the cool night air.

She whispers, we must pick up the pieces, build a safer bridge from
tonight to tomorrow.

With that he asks, where's that lean Cheetah with her green eyes & the
promise you made to keep us close?

& she retaliates, where's the prince of the jungle & his willingness to
abandon all things blue?

To which he concludes, I have nothing to share with history & closes
the silver box that holds his mask & wand.

The Extreme

Take me sister / as I am: one arm shorter / one testicle / one eye askew . . .

She whispers,

'Come darling. No matter. I need you / your tongue first, darling. I need your tongue.'

& he laughs & sticks it out & waggles it like a snake & touches his nose with it & his chin &

she laughs & cuddles in his arms like a cub in spring & licks his ear & asks, 'where will we be in October, my love & where will we be in May?

& he chucks her under the chin & says, 'In October we'll be in-carcerated, like a fox in a box. In May in-cinerated, like a squirrel on a spit.

& she laughs again & says, 'No. I'm not inclined to go where you have us jailed or charred – it's to bed with you or not.

& as he twirls his braided whip & curls an enraged fist she storms away & over the dunes &

he flaps his faithless arms & chases her to the brink where she is no longer but born again

in the seal's sleek & supple skin.

New Mexico Dreams

They're infused with suspicion: hammers & whips & no sign of relief. Remember, if the surface is slick you learn to chisel grooves:

Once, when Renee & I were young, she'd lifted me above her head like a bird ready for flight & airborne

we admitted our treachery & sins of omission. Later, home with a broken heart, she came to me & asked forgiveness.

Our next year was hell. No word from those she'd invited. We'd lost touch. Or so we thought. Once, a red dog appeared in flight.

Bitterness. That was the word. Bitterness & loathing. Those crippled by the fall from grace are always in need & then,

here come the recruiters, polished & brave who resemble our fathers but lack that sinister pleasure to judge.

April came & went. By July we were convinced there was no need for truth. Lies were the currency of survival.

& horses, always horses: Arabians, Appaloosas, Mustangs. Running. Across valleys, rivers, mountains.

Black & brown, dappled & cream. Racing against time & the confrontation with the 'other,' you know, the one with the missing arm, teeth askew,

the one with the reason to hate & hate he does. See. He's etched your face in the palm of his hand & waits

for the fire to catch & the cinders to blind your last good eye. You're merely meat & he'll toast you well.

Never forget the chase up the ladder to the loft. When you kicked him in the chest he went down & stayed there.

Forget the telephone that never stops ringing in the room you can never find. It was her. For sure. Or was it him again?
There are some questions best left unasked & those unanswered. Even the priestess with the necklace of bones will admit.

Take the keys when offered & don't look back. So many have been lost here. This neighborhood is cursed. Take a long last look & go.

It's Always – 'One Day At A Time'

". . . we go toward that moment / when we find out how we die . . ."

Galway Kinnell

From: "The Striped Snake And The Goldfinch"

Was it the blood-stained envelope under the door, a whispered insult at grandma Esther's wake, the wailing siren at noon?

Was it the currier with one good eye, the bartender who spiked your drink, the magician who disappeared?

Was it the moaning in the eaves, the pianist with six fingers on his left hand, the blind solider & his rusty harp?

Was it mother's last letter home, lipstick on your father's collar, the priest masturbating in the men's room?

Was it Lois who swam out too far, the snake that invaded the basement, Arthur's blood on your shoulder?

***

Maybe, the message, 'you're in dire straights' left on your answering machine, an unexpected chill in August, the dead duck in your mailbox?

Maybe, Carol's tempting offer of her bed @ midnight, Joel's broken nose & fractured jaw, the chipped dentures you found in the alley?

Maybe, scouring the street for your lost key, surviving the tornado, Angela's recounting of the time she was sold by her father to 'Uncle Joe?'

Maybe, the cave-in at the mine, living next-door to Andre who fed live chickens to his pit bulls, Jerome's photo of the mutilated corpse?

Maybe, erectile dysfunction, the cab that never came, orchids in winter, jasmine, honeysuckle, the broken plow, arsenic, an open knife, stones?

Into The Dark

There's a small girl with an automatic pistol & a man who drags an old woman in a basket.

There're two boys on horseback, one strums a guitar, the other recites the twenty-third psalm in French.

There've been many.

They claim they come for shelter & for food, for solace & for peace. The older men crowd the corners,

their kids smoke opium under the stairs, barter their women in the dank rooms above the bar.

& so it begins.

On the fringe of the park a gang of men with whips have cornered a woman. They

call her impur (unclean) & unleash the dogs. Her cries rip a ragged hole in the night.

Some have rebelled.

Whispers of bodies decomposing in the swamp, one, pregnant, found downstream, her baby dead.

Others have fled. The rutted road's alive with their sweat & excrement. Scrawled on the overpass:

Ici vit l'enfer (Here lives Hell).

At The End

I turn to the beginning. That time when possibilities clawed at our skin leaving welts like furrows where we could plant anything:

cotton, for the sheets on which we spread our bodies for hours of love & sometimes just sex for the sake of the act itself,

tobacco, for those late night sessions under the stars with brandy & coffee & talk of revolution & mayhem & visions of traveling on,

apples, for the fallow days of winter when neither you nor I spoke of the future or the past but were stuck wrestling with the descending cold,

spinach, for the salad to rival all salads with tuna & capers, Gorgonzola & almonds, currants & pinoles, lime juice & cold pressed olive oil,

tomatoes, red & yellow, large & small to suck on a hot June afternoon at the edge of a still lake where we'd dangle our bare legs & dream,

garlic, to heal the wounds we have & will inflict, not only those that run red but those that are too deep to surface willingly,

sweet peaches, for the last days of August when we lay on luscious beds of new mown grass & licked the juice that dripped from our sated lips,

& . . . gardenias, your mother's favorite, filling the house with their excess – one in your hair that afternoon the ship arrived to carry you away.

SPIDERS

You, Who Runs With The Dancers

in their hot red shoes, those collectors of knives who wrestle in alleys,
sleep
in junked jalopies, arrive above suspicion
ahead of the rest.

You, who ignores eruptions of blood, four white feathers, who floats
above
the town in sable & gold but poses clothed in khaki
in your palatial mirror.

You, who choked on the porridge of war, who studied Kabbalah, who lied
of planning your final ride with the sick & unwanted
on the train to oblivion.

You, who circles the house like the hunted bear trapped in the forest of
my
dreams, his heart, when they found him, still beat
in his cold clenched fist.

The Elephant In Our Closet

tramples years of assumptions & eats the green shoots that line the walls.
He's been our guest for a year or more. The shoots grow back each night.

He was left by a family heading west to the sea. The kids were upset.
On warm mornings, he treats himself to a swim in the pool. Lilacs.

Once, in a pensive mood, he talked of his childhood in Sri Lanka. As a calf,
he was free to wander with his mom but as he grew older there was work.

He hauled tons of wood & was beaten by his drunken keeper. One day,
he stomped the guy to mush & hitched a ride with a traveling circus.

The rest is history: train ride, boat ride, truck ride & our closet, the closest
to continuous safety he's known. Every few hours we top-up his water.

This week, he asked to relocate. We didn't press him but were curious. Is
there a problem here? Something we've done or not? Pool too small?

He needed to travel. Maybe, find a female. After all, he's a mature male with
desires. He's heard us talk of Portland, plenty of rain & lush grasses. &,

there's California, the movie studios. Always looking for exotic acts & curiosities. He promised to report on all that transpires. We helped him pack.

It Was The First Of The Year

For Judy Reeves – who knows where the wolves lie down

& we'd been waiting for the new moon to shed light on our neighbor
who smokes black cheroots &

straddles a wooden mustang left roadside by a passing carnival.
No one has gone to her.

It's unspoken.

*

The crows barked from the cottonwoods the day she stepped alive – stark
& naked from the carcass of the wolf,

the she-wolf, seen briefly in fall but heard to howl on snow-driven winter
nights wandering these hills calling her mate

dead four years – ambushed for the golden sword he wore.

Wolf-Woman, as she's called, doesn't speak of origins or history. It's
enough for her to rise in the night

often seen squatting in Cassiopeia's chair, stalking an irate Hercules or
scaling the long back of Draco the dragon.

Some say she copulates with Zeus but who would believe such lies.

We've left an offering of bones & bread. There's a man who plays the sitar,
others who sculpt her image &

dress her in straw – the fearful accuse her of bestiality & make the sign
of the cross.

Stories abound. There's little truth. You must not expect to see . . .

After: Kiki Smith – A Gathering – Whitney Museum – 2006-7

Spiders

It's the day we'd planned to leave. The spiders scuttle & wave where
we pass with our test-tubes & satchels.

They struggle to find a way into our plans as if they know we won't return
or (maybe worse) will deny them as we go.

Herman, he's the oldest, (or so we believe) paces from web to web
extracting strands & dead moths, tossing them

(along with the tidy bits you've helped to weave) where they clutter the path
– gossamer strands married to the flimsy red of your thread –

It's been a curious battle from the start. The garden's healing calm broken at
night – abuzz with their industry.

& your need to repair their fractured webs. Mon Dieu. What were you
thinking? The nights filled with their racket

as they swarmed to undo your meddling. One shimmering fiber at a time. &
Sarah, (we think of her as Herman's wife),

her blue-black sheen a startling contrast to nature's greens & grays,
scurrying to make repairs, to beat you at your game.

& now, this taking leave. Unity in shambles. Chased out, you might say,
by our broken bond.

Disgrace & distrust will follow. When the babies we've sequestered in a
small glass cage ball themselves in shrouds,

like enraged slaves they'll signal (as the others before them) death before
dishonor.

Their Chairs Remained

For Merrill Leffler

That afternoon they found their way from their terrace
through the forest of trumpet vines to this small patch of meadow
not already sown with those symbols of our family's passing.

As the sun slid south they sipped an aged Rioja, smoked their slim
Panatelas & summoned once again his capture in Changjin, her time
as whore for the Japanese. Nothing easy / never unholy / always sincere.

Age made little difference in their lives. The slightly older woman,
the younger man, war weary both. They took their time, each moment
as sweet as a plum, each gesture a gift of deliverance.

By sunset they were gone. Maybe to the river beyond the cottonwoods,
maybe to the chapel at the edge of town, maybe to wander in moonlight
among the monuments & stones that mark the rows.

Their chairs remained, as they'd left them, angled enough to face each
other & open enough to scout the woods & sky. There may be something
hungry loose – there may be little time left.

On Land & Under Water

Tobacco's in short supply, as is Rum. If my sister hadn't fucked that Swiss Guard for cash, we might have robbed our neighbors.

At night, when the tide ebbs, a Parrotfish will suck your fingers, weave its cocoon around your exposed body.

Times are tough. Don't laugh. We've survived on our reputation for violence & an innate ability to be redeemed.

If this is your first time, you will be told to leave your wife & sons, hunt with the Orcas or Great White.

She waited for him to finish his Highland Park & tagged him in the lot behind. "It would be her, the bitch," he was heard to say.

Don't be fooled. Accidents happen. Follow the Otters & the Seals; they know the place to sleep without fear.

Before boarding his last flight, he asked their forgiveness & was offered the choice of the dagger or the gun.

When you've been found free, the octopus will lead you to the white city under the bridge where your family waits.

"Spare my son, the traitor, he was never a willing partner." From a diary found in the desk of the executed Colonel.

Off the coast lies a lava-tube inhabited by a lazy Moray Eel & those lucky enough to have the blessing of the sea . . . we are of them.

When The Deaf Child Died

We who only value the future, what of the present? A life lived? Make no mistake, when you take his hand or hers / these are their days too.

Each stage of this life begins & ends / assumes a bridge from one to the next. To disallow the value of each crossing in its turn is to deny the whole.

*

I only wish it hadn't been at night. He couldn't see in the dark, couldn't see the voices of his trapped comrades.

*

Our time together was not always mad with orange blossoms, sunlight & laughter. No.

More tentative, like the Frigate Bird that soars on a rescuing wind, a spinning top

that merely marks its spot, lovers who seek release before they must begin again . . .

No. Our time was always measured by our son's

& his by the moving hands that keep the clock alive, raindrops that pelt a sky at sunset

too hot to hold or bruised w/frost . . . his mother's eyes that twinkled in her still white face.

We will never know the race he ran

between the trees, a pack of wolves at his heels, wooden sword in one hand, white rose between his teeth

& blood – to mark each step / one leg before the other / driven to see
what he could not hear.

We can only assume

as the ship rolled as the roll became a dive as the stern spun on its axis
as the smothering began

he must have known

like that pup who'd shuddered its last in his arms – like grandmamma
who tried to hold him high . . . the bridge to the next (as we've known it)

will not be.

After Tom Stoppard: The Coast of Utopia – Part 2 – Shipwreck

A Unicorn Crosses The Brooklyn Bridge

After a mysterious fog had descended on the city:
A bruised black hand with polished nails was found inside
          the carcass of a fallen lamb,
Auntie Sue was photographed running naked over rooftops
          in her frilled & flowered Easter Bonnet,
A man behind a turtle mask appeared at the out-of-the-closet
          party for Brother Timothy from Trinidad,
Grandma Esther's spirit was seen cloaked in a beaver coat sucking
          the toes of an isolated foot,
A female Japanese mannequin wrapped in a plastic shroud was hidden
          under a bench in Grand Central Station,
River rats scampered up & down the walls of Trinity Church to tease the
          Cardinal – too old & fat for flight,
In Battery Park detectives discovered a woman in mink drowned in a
          bathtub with a rubber duck,
Teenage boys & girls fucked all night on the manicured lawn of the
          Governor's summer home on the outskirts of Peekskill,
A mischievous unicorn was spotted prancing with tourists as they
crossed
          the Brooklyn Bridge at sunrise – on her back a sleeping cheetah
          above her head a brace of cooing doves.

The Resting Boxer

He poses on a rock apparently after a bout, elbows at rest on his knees, hands clasped, body & mind at ease after combat. He is naked except for a thong to protect his genitals. With broad shoulders & long limbs, a powerful chest & well-trimmed beard he has the bearing of a mature athletic man. A slight layer of fat at the waist hints at his aging. His swollen ears, right eye, nose & mouth tell of his beatings as does his bloody mustache & the drops of blood that have fallen on his right arm & leg.

She calls him Atlas after the god who led the Titans against Zeus & sketches him hauling the world on his back as the story tells. &

she dreams him in her bed where she bathes his broken face with kisses & his tortured body with her tears.

They've been lovers in another place – at another time, she's convinced & draws their coupling in charcoal & magenta.

Tonight she'll wait for him under the stars where he'd found her that first time, or so she remembers.

And because it was cold with wind & rain he'd wrapped her in his greatcoat & promised to calm the night.

From one season to the next & from wherever he was sent he would write or call, or so she remembers.

Solitary & brooding he cannot think to fulfill her expectations or those of his long-past youth.

Instead, he muses on the night's gambit where survival is the measure & failure must be held at bay.

If they are a mated pair, as she would have it, they must belie all odds: scatter roses if he's crowned – lilies if not.

The Resting Boxer From: Museo Nazionale Romano – Palazzo Massimo: Rome Italy

He Thinks Of Her

naked. Her broad hips welcoming. To be invited. To be folded in.
That would be a wild ride, until, she turns the corner & is gone.

Some days we get what we want or need or think we do.

Like that Thursday. Remember. It was raining & the car wouldn't start.
We climbed in back to be warm & steamed up all the windows.
It was then we swore 'never again in a back seat' – we're too old for this,
you said & besides we now have a bed at home & . . .

& then there are the days of wonder & deceit. You know these too.

It was Cape Cod in June & cement work was all I could find when you decided to take the job dancing for Mark & those guys at Viva La Noche also known by the common: Viva La Nooky. It was never the same after that. Sometimes I wonder, whatever happened to you?

& those days that appear without warning sucking the air out of time:

Zagreb. After the war, your one good leg wrapped around my back while I took my time, careful to keep us balanced, holding your pleasure paramount. You laughed after that. Warned me not to be too careful, warned me not to make a mockery of war & the objects left.

& the last days, those that imply the end, from which there is no escape:

They may come without warning, as did yours. Or, pose & flirt, hide & seek like my own. We know the past as a fantasy forever at risk of being caught in its lie, the present ephemeral at best, & the future, a mirage shimmering at the desert's edge, as seductive as Jezebel & equally treacherous.

It stays the same, these temptations, these urges with no bounds. Like . . .
thinking of her naked. Her broad hips welcoming. To be invited . . .

Acknowledgements

Grateful acknowledgement is made to the following journals and anthologies where these poems first appeared or are about to appear.

Free Lunch

The Usual Suspect

The Man & The Moon

I Saw Her Through The Mist

Magee Park Poets Anthologies - 2009/2010

Where Brothers Speak

If I Tell You The Truth

A Year in Ink Anthology Vol. 1 – 2008

You've Entered Their World

At Night All Cats Are Grey

He Tucks The Morning Line In His Hip Pocket

A Year In Ink Anthology Vol. 2 – 2009

On The Edge

The San Diego Poetry Annual – 2007

When The Deaf Child Died

The San Diego Poetry Annual – 2008

The Clock Strikes One

Where It All Began

Poets & Artists

At The End

Ocho

Their Chairs Remained

The Blue Moon Literary and Art Review

The Part Of The Gypsy Girl

Other Books By Roger Aplon

Stiletto

By Dawn's Early Light At 120 Miles Per Hour

It's Mother's Day

Barcelona Diary

The Man With His Back To The Room

Intimacies

Chapbooks

After Goya

Escapades

Improvisations

Homage To A Widow

Improvisation: After Debra Kaye's Changing Forms